Somewhere Between The Sand A

Joshua Van Leader

"For the past few years I have channelled all my grief and pain into my work. I just hope that it touches people and inspires them to keep fighting and keep going. You are exactly where you should be."

Joshua Van Leader

VOLUME III

Joshua Van Leader

BE A LIGHT THAT NEVER GOES OUT...

Let me burn for a little while,

Let me fight the inner pain,

Let me put the broken pieces

back to together, once again,

You can't see the infinite love I have,

And at times neither can I,

Even though I try,

I just feel broken,

It sometimes feels not enough,

But I care, I care deeply.

It's hard to fight, when I feel like a hurricane,

These memories shall burn in me

And I will land whenever and wherever I need to land.

Is it too much to ask for;

a stimulating conversation,

about our dreams and our passions,

what we fear? What we admire the most?

How far would you go for the things you love?

Maybe we finish each others sentences,

or we dance in the rain,

is it too much to ask for?

A love that never burns out,

constantly reignited,

and never the same.

Think of those that said you couldn't do it.

Think of those that said you're stupid.

Think of those that said you couldn't be great.

Think of all those idiots that said you were wrong.

When those doubts seep in, and when worries creep in,

Remember, DON'T GIVE UP.

You have all them to prove wrong.

Joshua Van Leader

You can't put a plaster on depression. It doesn't show bruises.
It hides away in the corners and whispers in the night.
Sometimes you don't even know it's there,
or more so why it's there. You can't look at someone
and see they are depressed because they can mask it.
It never discriminates, because it has no boundaries.
It can curse someone and the ripple effect of it is unimaginable
and it has infiltrated our society. So don't judge people
and just as importantly; listen more. Feel the need to be kinder,
and instinctively; try to be understanding.
Because we never know what each other is going through
and we never know, an act of kindness or a simple smile can
change the course of someones history,
maybe even your own.

FIND YOUR SPACE

They sighed and whispered.....

"Take me back.

To where the fountains of Versailles pour over me

and I glisten in the sunlight.

Take me back to where I shimmer.

To where the golden hour is enough.

Living is proof that my own affirmation is enough."

DRAW A MAP
TO GET LOST

100 ASPECTS OF THE MOON

Try to refrain from talking so much to someone who struggles
with depression in such a way that they are not speaking,
They don't need advice all the time, try to listen instead.
Because they may have so many other voices racing around in
their head, they may have thoughts consuming their very
existence, contemplating how to escape them
can be the reason they are so silent.

Imagine falling short of the mark
Falling into the sea
Into its hidden parts
Where nothing happens
There is stillness
There is a darkness like oblivion
There is no hope
There is nothing but fear
That is how depression can sink you.
It engulfs you.
You are not alone, you have a good fight in you.

Speak out.

Perhaps if you see yourself for what you can be;
be a kinder person.
Be a person that carries an essence of kindness,
throughout your tiny history on this planet,
you will never regret being kind
and not that it matters;
you will always be loved for it too.

l'appel du vide
53.9921° N, 1.5418° W

Maybe you are destined to be at war.

Destined to be sat at the table in a battle with adversity.

It's painstakingly difficult and sometimes you stand alone.

But my oh my, when you fight on as you are,

fight on and conquer this temporary struggle,

the peace you will find, the love you will embrace

and the strength you posses will shatter

and break boundaries you didn't even know existed.

You will no longer just exist because of this adversity,

you will thrive.

Tribute

She craves freedom.

She craves the ocean air and the taste of salt water on her lips,

She craves the stillness and calm wind at dusk,

The cold morning swim,

She goes a little crazy for the moon and the stars

and books that make her feel melancholy,

She's a hive of adrenaline packed into one,

even a little wild and bright like the sun.

There is a lot of maybes, tonnes of ifs,

Many tomorrows and countless yesterdays,

Masses of ups, and a great deal of downs,

Many mountains and even fewer seas

Yet with all that said, there's just one of you.

What a rare combination, of matter, of stardust

and atoms it took to build something so unique,

yet so temporary. Make the most of you.

For that is all there is and ever will be again.

And if that isn't magic or art,

then I don't know what is.

IT'S NOT MEANT TO BE **GOOD**.

Life is never meant to be just 'good'.

It's supposed to be gripping and thrilling.

Its meant to challenge you,

for you are here to excel yourself,

to paint your canvas in whatever hues you so wish to choose.

It's meant to ignite part of you that you didn't know existed.

It's that ever evolving process that is the stigma for life.

escape the ordinary

Some people think that to write or enjoy poetry and art

you must be a romantic or a dreamer.

But the truth is much darker than that

You must know pain at first hand,

and perhaps suffer solitary or feel alone,

at some point you were possibly a cynic,

There is a lot to be said

for all the adversity you endure to appreciate an art form

There is intelligence and wisdom,

but also an understanding of how much pain

Someone has gone through

to write or create what they have done,

It may not be pretty, but ironically that is the beauty of it all.

I hope one day you find your voice like I have.

I hope you know how important you have been

to help me find mine again.

But this voice of mine was broken once.

I had to find the courage to continue,

the willingness to accept help.

You have to enjoy the small wins,

accept your reality but always keep a bit of crazy in you,

the world will always need abstract minds.

53.9921° N, 1.5418° W

icarus flew

OTHER PERSPECTIVES

I forgot who I was once.

I thought that maybe I am a man not worth knowing,
that I was finished and should be forgotten about.
I wasn't relevant anymore.
But then I remembered I have a story worth telling,
and a man who has a story worth telling
is always a man worth knowing.

TO DEFINE IS TO LIMIT

When your mind is tired of fighting against itself,

your legs feel every step, heavy and weak,

your eyes flicker with exhaustion

and you feel that it's not going your way,

then is the pivotal moment that you've anticipated all these years.

You're on the brink of something,

you won't know if it's something spectacular,

or something tragic, but you have to be here to witness it,

you must be prepared.

You have to open your soul

to acceptance of failure & falling,

for you can withstand it.

You have to be fierce yet patient,

then instinctively, you just have to go for it.

There are no rules,

but you must create your own guidelines.

We're all caught up in our small problems.

Here on this spinning rock,

here in this unique moment of time,

here where miracles are happening all around us,

going almost unnoticed, the chances of your very existence

are that of a grain of sand on our beaches.

Fixate on your dreams,

worship the universe,

imagine your reality;

and it will be so.

Art allows me to run away
from the tragedy of reality.
It allows me
to escape this world for another,
so don't ever think
art is not as important as other matters
or as influencial as other subjects,
it saved my life,
and it did so,
more than once.

PARADOX

What are we to do if not bleed?
I am told talking about this suffering and pain helps,
but whenever I do
I only feel judged and embarrassed, even guilty at times,
these emotions are not mine,
I feel foreign trapped in this skin,
I don't understand how I got here?
Am I to accept this pain to be my future?
Am I not to live a different life than what I have?
Who am I?
What am I to do but bleed, cry and crumble?

She was a fortress really,

her walls reached high with hope,

and the moat around her was filled with kindness.

She was a castle inside and out.

But even more so like the sea.

Creatively poetic,

undeniably

an enigma.

different eyes
see different things

CALYPSO

There is no second life.

There is no chance to do this all over again.

That is why it is tragic you waste your time,
yet beautiful you remember this lesson.

for you will not waste another moment
once you realise it's all we've got.

Drink it all in, this poison won't last.

When we are apart,

the sky burns on fire,

and so does

a part of me.

I have got better without you,

but it still hurts.

Be intoxicated by the mysterious,

stay away from the vulgar,

live your life in such a way that to some it may seem strange,

stare at the stars too long,

admire the ocean wholeheartedly,

you owe no one anything,

you only owe yourself the gift

of an eventful, inventive and creative life.

TO DEFINE IS TO LIMIT

Inception

/ɪnˈsɛpʃ(ə)n/

noun

the establishment or starting point of an institution or activity.

Her mind poisoned herself with daggers,

like the raining crashing down in the green garden outside,

but its black, there is no moon tonight,

the stars are hiding again,

the soft piano sound of Debussy calms her emotions

there was only artificial light from her bedside lamp

that merely flickered in the corner,

the hope was damp,

but something stirred within her

that this time will pass, just like the rain,

and she must be ready for that time,

she asked herself, what do I have to do to be prepared?

We all can learn a lesson from the rain....

2014
" REVOLUTION REVIVAL "

Write one good thing down a day,

and in 365 days you have yourself a book.

Make one good decision a day,

and in a year,

you are closer

at being your own hero.

Every human has some form of spark of genius within them,

it is not up to the world around us to ignite it,

you can't sit in your room,

or hide in a hole for that to happen,

you need to get out there, make mistakes, tread on thin ice,

nothing good will come to you immediately,

and when it does,

it may appear distorted,

but everything we create at first is always a little blurred,

it is up to our bit of genius to sharpen the sense,

to burn down the temporary window or mediocracy.

We need to lose the fear of being mysterious

and welcome it insted.

Sometimes, you are already great.

You're already good enough.

You are already well trained and versed, you're prepared and ready.

Sometimes it isn't anyone else holding you back.

Sometimes you are the only obstacle getting in your way.

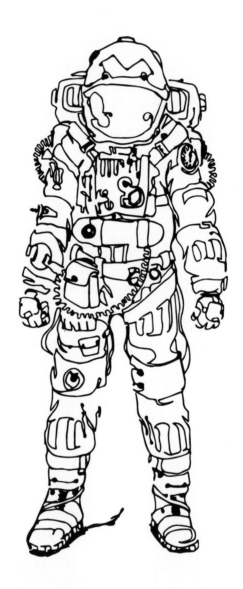

DREAM OF STANGER WORLDS

She always had

this intoxicating look in her eye,

that would mirror that of the sky.

Sometimes, it was a sunrise,

sometimes a sunset,

sometimes a starry night.

Don't be a reflection of your emotions,

be a definition

of the courage you have to fight them

There will always be someone that doesn't like you.

There will always be someone who doesn't like what you create.

There will always be someone who is jealous of you.

But there is nothing you can do about that,

when you realise that,

your solitary becomes peace

and your dreams become unstoppable.

DEFINE BRILLAINT.

DEFINE MADNESS FIRST.

Art is ever evolving, just like nature.

That is why nature

will always be the most substantial inspiration for art,

and our most significant enigma.

We must admire and embrace nature.

Because nature is the poetry of life.

I've considered suicide.

Romantacised death.

The dark wolf on my shoulder whispiered

about the peace in the blackness of oblivion.

I no longer feared but welcomed it.

The scars on my body

seemed to of faded now.

I loathe the scars that I am decorated in.

As horrid as they look and as scarred as I am,

they are mine.

The symbolize bravery,

and the courage I will always possess.

The tragedy was

that my heart raced for you,

like a raging comet,

but you never cared

to look up

and admire the stars.

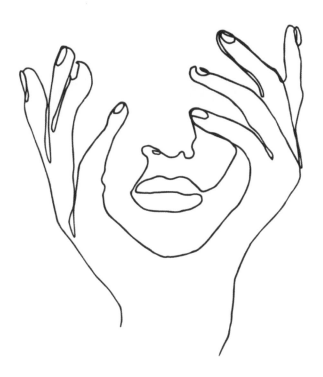

Joshua Van Leader

THINK PEACE, TEACH PEACE, LOVE PEACE

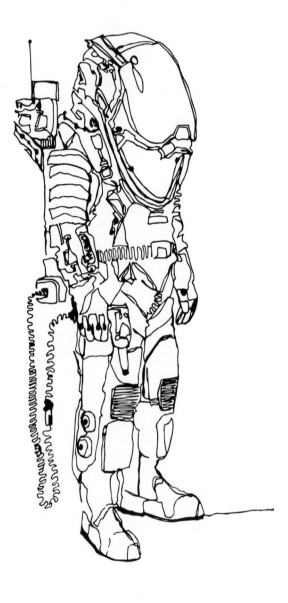

I want to communicate my pain

and suffering into a different dimension,

but it's difficult explaining something unexplainable,

how do you take out the pain that is so engrossed into my blood,

I have to get it out, but how?

So I am rid of the terror that haunts me at night,

the black wolf that howls throughout my mind,

I need to communicate it through my work,

not because it is relevant,

but because it is inescapable,

and therefore inevitable.

It's all very good knowing want you don't want.

Defining what we don't want is easy,

it's what you do want that counts.

It's being able to pin down,

knowing precisely what we want that truly matters.

DRAW A MAP TO GET LOST. CIRCA 1947

I have a strong pull towards the ocean.

It is such an enigma,

yet I feel a powerful connection to it.

I am at peace whenever I am there.

The air always tastes better by the sea.

The sounds there are of euphoria,

I am in a state of delight there,

a calming state of happiness,

almost dreamlike.

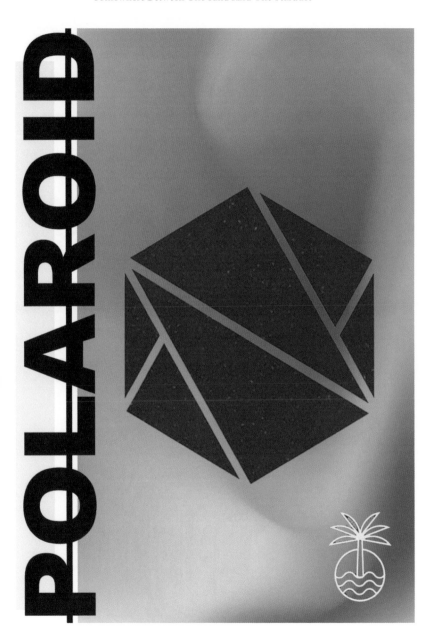

be an enigma, have a sense of mystery about you....

Perhaps we want to be understood first,

then loved.

Or maybe we want to be respected and well thought of,

and then loved.

For a vigorous foundation like those,

are a good beginning to love and be loved.

I want to carry myself like an iridescent mythical creature,

I don't want to be defined by a few short words,

or explained in a boring sentence.

I want to entice people, I want to be extraordinary.

I want my work to fill up peoples minds

and transcend them to another world,

I don't want to just be admissable,

I want to burn souls with rapture and passion,

I am intoxicated by the idea of my work being brilliant,

I do not settle at average.

It's about fighting for something.

Finding something that makes you want to rest at night

so in the morning you can go attack it.

Find something that you are so passionate about

that you fear losing it.

It's existence thrills you.

You have to find it,

because it compels you to develop,

and that is what you need to feed your soul.

That is what we stay alive for.

We are suffering in some unearthly way,

we are faced with adversity, time and time again,

but we never say

"I need this.

I need this pain for my character building.

I need solitary

I need to burn a little while

and come back reborn, time and time again."

Joshua Van Leader

HOPE

In a way,

she was a mystery,

even when I knew her well enough,

she was some kind of magical spell to me

I was cast and thrown in

to her world of fascination for beautiful things,

and on dark lonely nights

she gave me hope, light and love.

If people were nature,

I was a grain of sand,

And she was a mountain.

I have thoughts that come to spoil me,

bit by bit. Little by little,

they chip away at my fragile state of mind.

I'm vulnerable at night

and it's as if the thoughts know that too.

They plan a way to enter my mind with complexities

and crowd my judgement

they supply one another,

they leave me broken, drained and weak.

Then they run into the night sky

among the stars, they camouflaging themselves,

only to come haunt me the next day.

That is why I feel destined to be at war with myself,

and the fight goes on, into the morning...

Stare into the stars for too long.
Get lost up there.
But make sure to come back,
and be careful when you do.

Reality can be dark,
and rather depressing,
especially when you realise,
it feasts on your dreams.

You will do well

to remember;

that it will be magical,

believe in yourself.

This should always

be at the forefront of any creative project.

This should be the title

of your mind every morning.

HAVE PEACE IN YOUR DREAMS

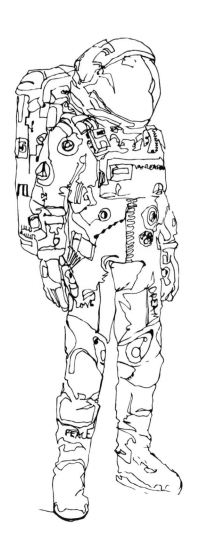

AND CHAOS IN YOUR ART

My moon is tired,

my sun has died out,

the stars are drunk,

and my universe is folding in on itself.

It doesn't seem to love me anymore,

in fairness; it owes me nothing,

but it still gives me something.

It gives me hope even in my darkest hours,

fills me with passion, with drive,

shows me strength in this battle with tyranny....

For so long, I've watched the sea in all its forms,

in all its decorated glory, with its tragical dawns,

I shed away part of my past,

the salt water heals me, I feel free,

I thought I would never last,

but hear I am, head above water,

stronger than ever, reborn of bricks and mortar,

I was once drowning, I shuddered in my peril,

locked myself away, like an animal in a kennel,

I gave up on myself, lost all good moral,

as nature saved me, not fading like white coral,

and I confess, I am afraid of my own mind,

I must fight on with courage and strength

for that I must find,

the tale does not end here,

like the ocean I go on,

without any fear,

I am still here.

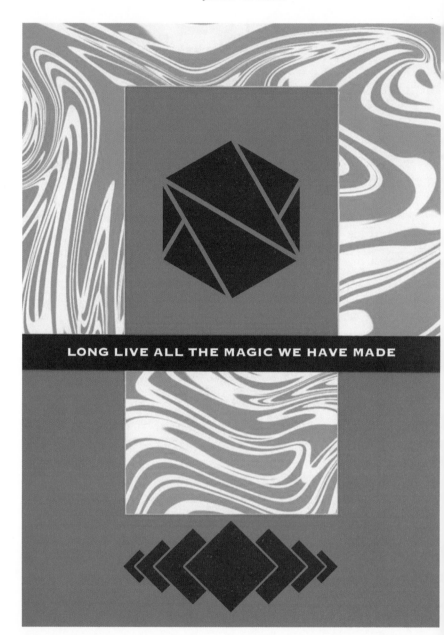

LONG LIVE ALL THE MAGIC WE HAVE MADE

She was a road map of creativity,

she was a radiant melody

an endless poem, beautifully written,

she was in harmony with elegance,

she rhymed day and night,

her attitude was arresting,

she will always remind me

of all these delightful and ethereal things.

WILD THINGS HAPPEN IN SILENCE

You are as educated as you are mistaken,

you are as beautiful as you are broken,

you have never been more alive than this moment,

that you realise you are a mosaic of beautiful tragic memories.

Maybe you are meant to be exactly where you are right now
The thing you are searching for
and insisting that you need;
it may come to you,

Or it may not.

Maybe on your journey and search you will grow
and find something greater than what you first imagined.

I did love you.

Maybe part of me always will.

But maybe not,

maybe I will be strong enough

to destroy that part of me

without hurting myself anymore.

Maybe you are meant to be exactly where you are right now

the thing you are searching for

and insisting that you need it may come to you,

or it may not.

Maybe on your journey and search you will grow

and find something greater than what you first imagined.

This page was repeated for a reason....

Part of me died that night,

and it is really easy for me to look

at all the negatives that were just demolished

in one evening.

It is really upsetting for me to look back

at what I had lost,

but even though part of me was gone,

a new part of me was reborn.

Joshua Van Leader

DIFFERENT EYES

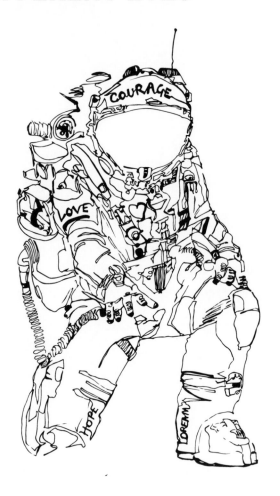

SEE DIFFERENT THINGS

I'll wrestle my worries, and throw my dreams into the stars,

and maybe they'll listen, and help tonic my scars,

these emotions I carry are only temporary,

and just once more, my character is tested,

I have tiresome struggles, so I must be better rested,

as I smile and inhale, another sea air breath,

I fight onward again, against this realm of death,

one hand full of stardust,

the other of strength,

may you find inspiration in all that you do,

I'm here for the climax, let us start anew.

It is a difficult thing...

To create or write your way out of hell
into liberation as it is often overlooked.
Imagine constantly feeling like it's pouring rain only over you,
when your legs feel heavier than a tonne of bricks,
and for no reason either, you just feel heavy,
you can't see the light for the clouds lingering over your eyelids,
and all you want to do is drop into a quiet sombre sleep...
But you continue to have the courage to fight against it,
this external darkness that has found its way into you,
the patience to respect your own process,
and the valour to accept that this is your life right now,
it is so brave to do so...
That is the truest philosophy you will ever live by.

And that is ok...
to walk through the valley of fear every single day
knowing it maybe your last.
Not because anyone else can take it from you,
this is the eerie part of it:
That you can take it from yourself, the urge you have to end it all
is overwhelming, and there is a homesickness for another world,
but you go on and on against the tides, on and on some more.
Alas, this is not a calling into the void,
this is your inception of brighter beginnings,
perhaps not today or tomorrow,
but you will get there, you will find a brighter side of the moon,
you will find your brilliance, your light, your hope.
But you have to be willing to walk through the darkness first.

I look at her

and wonder

where does she hide all the madness

all the fires and raging storms

that swirls around inside her?

Beauty like hers

is never born in flower gardens.

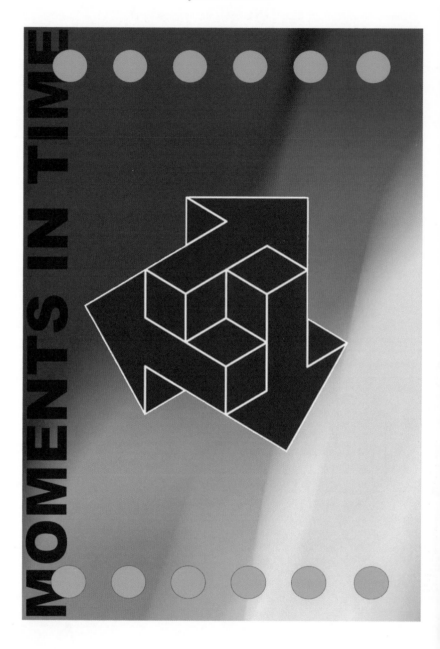

Seaboard and Forshore

It is on nights like this,

when the starlight sparkles,

and the shimmer of their lights,

hum across the top of the water,

the calm sea, like glass,

with the waves effortlessly brushing against the beach,

and the moon illuminates the scene,

the sound of the birds calling in the distance,

with the sound of the water tapping the side of the boats,

there is something ethereal about this image,

something cryptic,

it is a feeling,

and it will always be,

one of my favourite places to visit,

when I am in the darkest of my hours.

I will go there, time and time again.

5.15 am

I feel; worried, burnt...

I have no one else to speak to,

I'm scared of my own self,

I feel irrelevant,

like I'll end up on a shelf,

this self destructive and spiteful person

has plagued my thoughts,

and made the problems worsen,

how much more worry,

can one person take,

as I sit and wander into darkness,

my ego whispers "This is fake".

My character knows

to fight these foes,

for these emotions are temporary,

Inception! So the story goes....

BE AN ELIXER TO YOUR OWN LIFE

I like the Autumn.

It's so honest.

It is as if nature is saying,

I need a rest, a rebirth,

a chance to rejuvenate myself for another year.

The wonderful colours

that spark out

from all the different shades of green and blue of summer

are now taken over,

by splashes of red, orange and yellow,

and they clash with the darker blues

of the cold and early nights.

It is nature being poetic.

It is nature in its finest form.

When you create art,

don't hide the madness.

Don't hide the pain.

It isn't art if it isn't true and without reason.

You have to bring forward all that hurt

in order of it to have feeling.

It isn't to make sense and be easily understood,

it is supposed to have emotion, desire and mystery.

So create;

and bring forth the madness and chaotic art,

your soul needs it.

**BABYLON STUDIOS
PORTABELLO ROAD
LONDON**

Some people have to create in order to escape,

create another world, maybe one glamorous or charming,

maybe chaotic and weird,

but we need to release this suffering somehow,

how we are sins of our own faults,

we are to blame for our dreams,

if them dreams are too big,

you can't just expect people to all be the same,

we need people of abstract minds to bring us colour,

keep us on our toes too,

give our souls meaning,

you have to be able to get away from reality for a little while,

and interpret the world you see fit,

create, imagine and bring forward your light.

For without it,

this world would just be dull and grey.

We need your peculiarity and chaotic brilliance.

Falling short of something doesn't matter,

it takes a shot at your ego,

but not of your character.

It tests your character,

it tests how badly you want something,

how far will you pursue something you love.

Will you chase it to end of an ever going world?

Will you believe in it when no one else does?

It is supposed to test you,

it is supposed to be a paradox to you,

you have to be a little crazy about it

for others to believe in it.

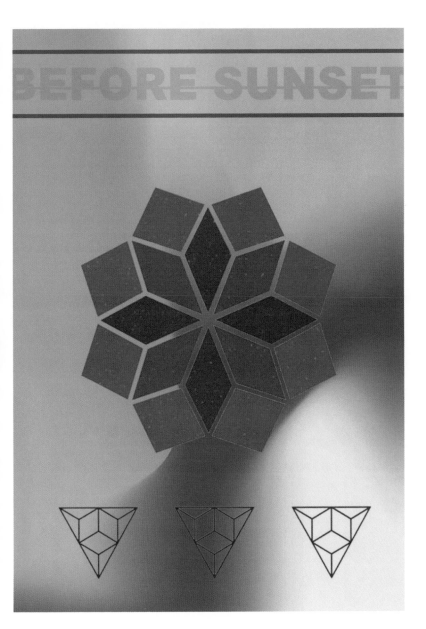

Never have I felt so vile towards myself,

depression is a difficult fight,

it saps and drains my health,

it lingers long after and often it is ugly,

it is not proof of who you are,

it is what's inside us that matters,

I can't give up, for I have come this far,

there is still a fight inside me,

my gates are open, my temples crumbled,

but I still hang to hope to set me free.

Being able to make sense of the world is a git.

Not all creature are as fortunate as you to see the it world like you.

Not everything feels the waves of life as thoroughly as you do.

If you ever wanted to be reminded that your life is unique,

just taste the ocean on your lips,

handle sand in your palm,

smell the wind,

look at the stars,

open the gates of your senses,

we all see and feel things differently,

be in touch with nature,

and it will talk back.

Don't think and focus on what you do not have.

Value and appreciate what you already have,

what you have overcome,

and more importantly,

the adventures that lie within you,

the stories you are about to create,

be excited about the things that lie ahead.

It is autumn in London;

the streets are packed with people in love,

in love with the city, in the love with the chill in the air,

the radiant city streets vibrate and the ambience it holds,

is romance in itself.

Their hearts are captured,

by trees that scatter through the city that flourish in burnt orange,

and scarlet reds and are now retiring

for the ice cold winter silently approaches,

but there is a warmness about it.

It is all happening right in front of everyone.

It's all so alluring, but only for a moment.

I think of you again

and even the busy, bewitching and romanticised

streets of London are not enough to fill in the void that is you.

I miss you terribly, most earnestly and enticingly,

I miss you.

I wouldn't say I fell in love with you by chance.

It happened so effortlessly.

Out of it all,

my favourite thing to do;

was seeing you smile

and knowing that it was because of me.

There were stories about you and I.

In books, in poems,

in art that hung on the walls of great museums,

in movies watched by all,

we were etched into others stories,

others dreams.

We were not just together,

I see us in every story;

that every artists ever told.

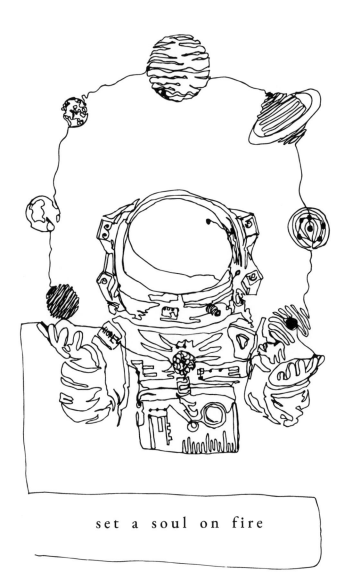

set a soul on fire

I have never really chased,

you have never really stayed,

and time

it seems;

has never really waited.

The way you love someone,
speaks volumes about the way
you love yourself.
That is why it is so important,
to love yourself
before anyone else.

REPEAT.

CREATE ART AND YOU BECOME ETERNAL

Talk to me about the weather,

tell me what you see in that painting,

tell me how that song makes you feel,

tell me what you dream of

when you glance upon the skies at night.

Tell me everything the way you see it.

I want to know how things influence you,

how you view the world,

what you love,

and how you want to be loved.

You can't write or create for other people.

You have to do it for yourself,

nobody wants to read or see

what they already know

or have seen before.

People want to be captured, ruptured

amazed by new ideas.

Let me

look

into your eyes

again,

give me

that fleeting feeling

of flying.

Joshua Van Leader

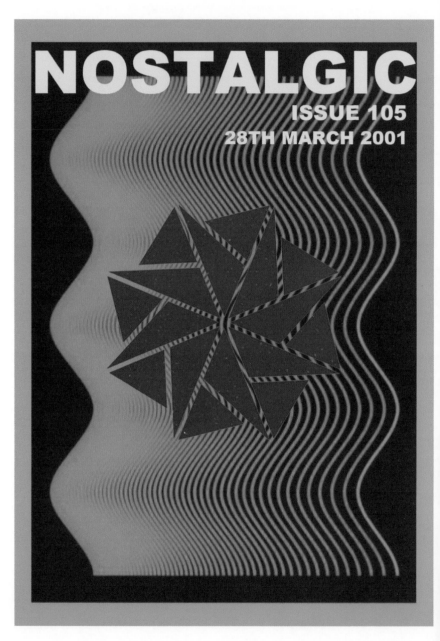

NOSTALGIC

ISSUE 105
28TH MARCH 2001

Nobody creates to just make money.

We create to fill a void or escape oblivion.

A void of pain,

a whirlpool of depression,

a sea full of raging anxiety

or a heart ruptured and torn.

Nobody creates to make sense.

We do it to heal,

to let out all that we feel inside,

so that we don't die from within.

She is taking me somewhere beautiful,

somewhere I feel that I belong,

somewhere between the sand and the stardust,

we are ascending together.

Around us, the stars are falling lanterns

we are among them, part of them,

touching our soft skin,

we are ascending deeper.

With her hand in mine,

are we falling or are we flying?

We seem to glue together so well,

assuringly, tightly, ardently,

we have been through the darkness together.

With her I am not afraid,

I don't feel alone, I am at home with her,

for her;

I am willing

to plunge into the beautiful unknown.

See yourself as a canvas,

and create the hell out of it.

Be carfeul what you say to other people,

your words can derail a person

from good thoughts in their solitude,

but equally;

you can set a light inside them,

and make them feel

that they can battle everything.

THIS FEELING
OF HOMESICKNESS
HAUNTS ME

CONSUME ME.....

With stardust pouring through my heart,

and stardust coursing through my veins,

I love, love, love.

I too feel it.....

I am scared of myself,
my brain,
the constant thinking
and cancer of depression,
such tenebrosity should only exist in hell.

YOU ARE EXACTLY WHERE YOU ARE MEANT TO BE

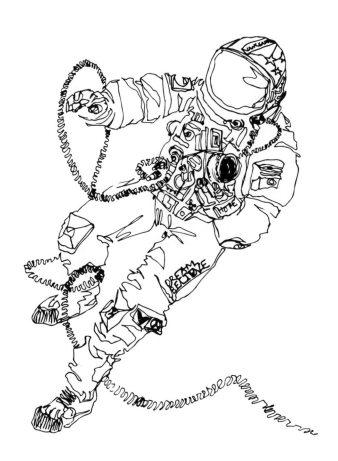

FLOW IN TUNE WITH THE UNIVERSE

I have scars that run deep
into my veins,
they can't be seen on this nervous surface,
nor can they be heard.
They don't heal,
they won't wash off,
they tire me,
for they are voices whispering at night,
and they are cunning.
It is easy to forget
that someone, somewhere
is suffering like this too.

MAKE
SOMEONE
ELSE
HAPPY,
NOT
FOR
YOURSELF,
BUT
FOR
THE
SIMPLE
FACT
THAT
IT
IS
THE
RIGHT
THING
TO
DO.

I think

we all nurse part of ourselves,

that we are afraid to show.

But the broken parts of us all,

is always the most interesting.

Often; there is a story there,

beautiful yet beguiling,

profound yet tragic.

Sometimes,

we look to others for hope,

inspiration or beauty.

Yet how many times have we reached

into ourselves

to be curious and bewildered

about what we have

swirling around inside of us?

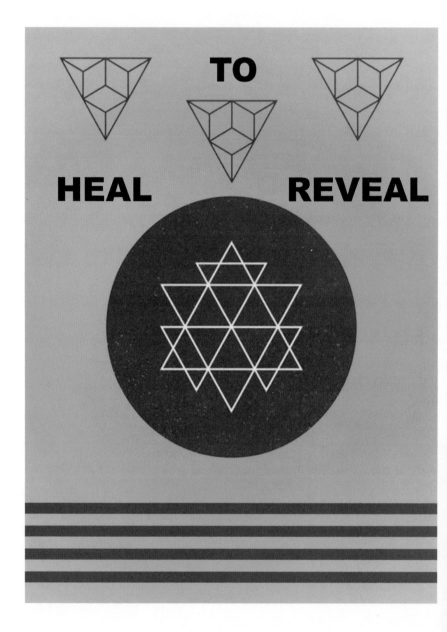

Endurance is paramount when creating.

The artist must have stamina.

But stamina and endurance are practised over time,

and they cannot be taught,

they must be lived.

Emotional suffering

can be a terrible fire.

It either purifies or destroys.

Yet it is not a chance to self destruct,

but an apportunity,

to come alive.

Live and breathe

your hopes and dreams.

That's what you want, isn't it?

Your mind and instinct are talking

directly to you.

Other people live in dreams,

but it is rarely their own.

Live your life as a brave dreamer,

one day at a time......

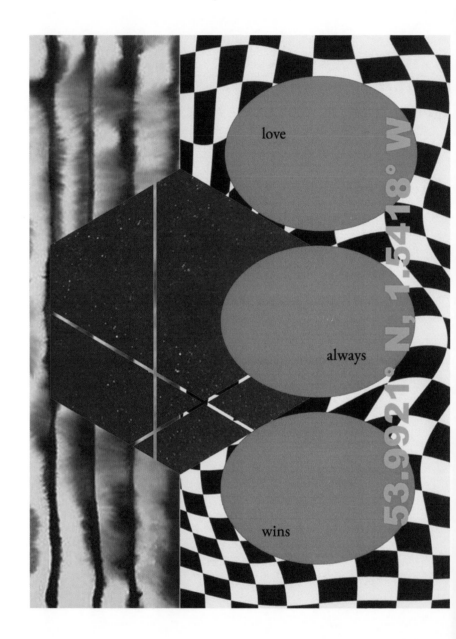

Creating something new is always daunting.

Some of what I write and create will be tossed aside.

But if we never have the courage to put it out into the world

how will we ever know? What a terrible waste,

of a beautiful life it would be to waste time on worry and doubt.

Nothing great was ever achieved by artists that remain silent.

Don't you agree?

It is a truly remarkable and wonderful moment
when you admire the nature of the world
and how it comes around full circle.
How wild it is.
Giving and taking.
Falling and rising.
It is a poem of balance.
Try and live in tune with it all.
Be a part of the art.

One day,

I will write poetry about this pain.

How it has tormented me,

four countless, horrible nights,

that seemed never ending.

About how it stripped me

of my dignity,

and strained me of my thoughts.

The depression exhausted me,

pushing me to face my own oblivion.

But for now, this small verse will have to do.

One day,
I will write poetry about you.
But right now,
I cannot.
For I am too busy loving you,
too busy spending my nights
under the stars with you,
counting our days together
and being so excited to be beside you
that it thrills me,
we are living our lives together
so vicariously and naturally.

Think like the minority,

yet remember,

be in touch with the majority.

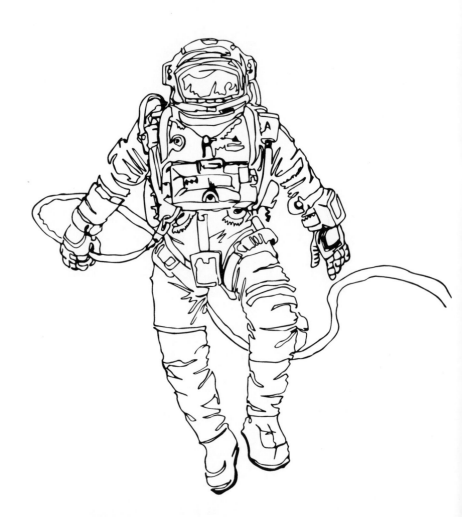

DON'T GET IN YOUR OWN WAY

Campaign of 1991...

I have had to learn the hard way
to fight myself,
by myself,
for myself.
Never the less,
I still learned,
and still am learning.

CREATE TRUE.

BE HONEST IN YOUR WORK,
BE BOLD,
DON'T EVEN TRY TO BE BRILLIANT,
JUST CREATE WITH EMOTION AND FEELING,

ALWAYS BE TRUE.

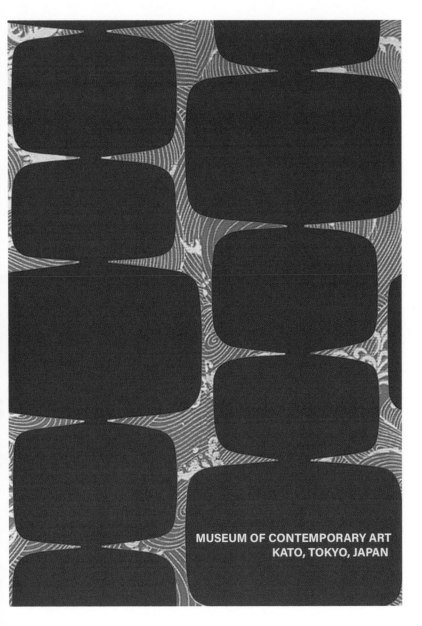

MUSEUM OF CONTEMPORARY ART
KATO, TOKYO, JAPAN

Be careful not to under estimate
how much energy transitions take.
It is easy to crumble and fade
into your own shadow,
neglecting your basic needs.
Transitions take energy.
Energy takes time and manifestation.
Remember that transisitons need to be respected,
or you will lose sight of what is truly important.

sometimes, believing is enough

Butter Jokes - Truths Hurt

It's true you know, everythings happens for a reason.

However,

more often than not,

the reason is because you made a stupid choice

and bad decisions,

and you are sometimes,

just an idiot for that.

But it doesn't mean you are not a good perosn,

it just means you were a little stupid.

There is nothing wrong dwelling in uncertain times,
It is only a problem when you are rooted within them,
Always carry the idea of progress,
no matter how slow it may be.

I just want to make a positive impact on the world.

I want to inspire at least one person to believe in their purpose or inspire them to come close to peace within themselves.

I want to help someone, even help them help.

I just want to leave a ripple effect of positive waves.

Don't you?

Who do you think of when you look up
to the stars?

The answer will say a lot about who you miss
and truly care about.

It is I on this boulevard,

it is I who walk these streets,

these terrifying streets that lead into darkness.

It is I who walk on this boulevard,

it is I who holds my head down on these avenues,

these avenues of self doubt and comparison.

Is it I who fails I,

or is it the enviroment I am part of?

It is I who fight for I,

on this road of solitary.

It is I who define the path of my own fate,

and I who has the bravery to accept the change of it,

no matter how difficult, it will not change my trait.

It is I, yes I, who has the patience to wait,

for art, love and beauty will always defeat this hate.

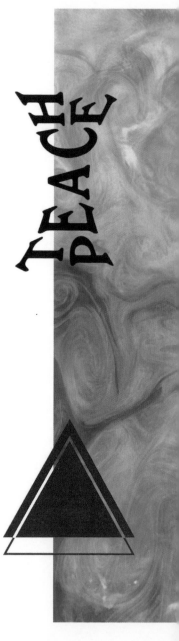

Some mornings, afternoon, evenings and especially nights
are just too much. I do not exist at times. I am in that moment
forgotten. I am defeated. I can not explain it with spoken words.
So, I am compelled to writing it down. I am withdrawn and no
matter how I try to ignore my own thoughts, they drown me
until I am suffocated by them. I am a museum, a sad proverb,
but at least 'I am' and that is enought to fight for.

I have felt it too...

Can you give me an idea of how you are feeling?

I can't tell you exactly, but I can give you an analogy.
I feel like Icarus. I have flown to close to the sun,
I hve flown close to the scorching sun and I am burning.
I am falling, I am a blaze,
and soon I will be dust.

There is this energy she gives off.

This radiant energy,

it's like an unknown planetary exploration with her,

you're on this exciting adventure

and you're so happy she's alive.

All you want to do is dive into the stars with her,

and keep floating from star to star.

Believe

You have a powerful enigma at work within you,

I mean, you are a galaxy of imagination,

and an intellect crammed precisely into a spec of dust,

with infinite dreams and a boundless sky of stars,

all floating around in your head.

it is both frighteningly dangerous,

yet extraordinarily prolific.

Don't give me long words or nice things.

That is for kings and queens,

I am just a regular human being;

I want you to test me, excite me, and lets flourish together.

I want to try and connect with you

talk to me about mystical things,

like other worlds and sand and stardust.

Does the vast ocean scare you?

Does the endless sky make you think?

Does the ocean make you happy?

Do the mountains free you?

You need to find a place

that makes you fill the void,

but in an uplifting way,

find the place that brings

an untroubled kind of solitude.

We compare ourselves to others.

We make ourselves think

that we are not doing a well as them.

Or maybe it is the other way around;

that we are not as sick as them.

But surely that is a sign

of sickness and ill health.

You need to comfort yourself,

give yourself grace and do not harm yourself,

the world is already

trying hard enough to do that to you.

Your worth and happiness

can be taken away

if you don't respect it,

people are out there

that want what you have,

and human beings

naturally will take it too.

They will not appreciate it fully,

and it will ruin you both

but in different ways.

So protect what you have,

because it may be taken away from you,

and you will have no idea

that you are losing what you love

right under your nose.

I have always been ashamed of the way I think.

My thought process isn't ideal.

It isn't as efficient as I would have hoped,

and it tires me to the floor, the dirty begrimed floor.

but I appear to keep fighting back,

to clean that floor up,

and rise,

rise and rise again.

EIGENLICH WOLLTE ER NIE EIN EIN LIEBESLIED

165

Do not diguise your pain,

in loving someone else,

it will only create more pain,

it will only ever erupt

in a brutal way of life.

I am writing once again.

I am lonely in this world of billions,

how is that possible?

Hammering lonliness and isolation

into my keys.

I am a tragedy of rejection

and seclusion,

my soul has witnessed abandonment

and ice now runs through my veins,

layer by layer,

I am vanquished by it.

Joshua Van Leader

THERE IS ALWAYS HOPE

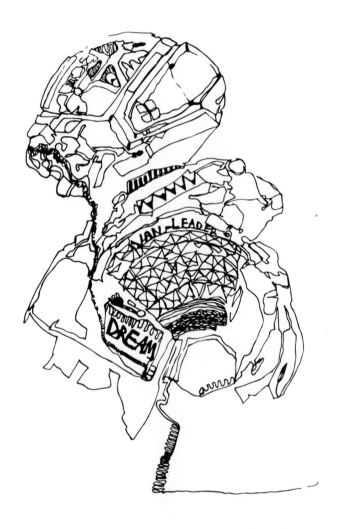

To create consistenly

is not an easy endeavour,

it is full spectacles,

a drama that consists of self doubt and struggle,

but it means there is fight still left in you,

some voice, somewhere within you

that murmurs;

"We are still here,

fighting to the very end."

Your mind must listen to your body

and body must listen to your mind.

If there is a conflict there,

then it will be weary and tiresome.

It must be a coordinated effort,

for if it is balanced correctly,

be ready for a grand adventure.

23 Parliament Street,
Harrogate, North Yorkshire,
HG1 2QU

Too many times I have not had the valour to write,

paint, sing or create how I wish.

I have been a convict to my own personal prison,

screaming at myself without ever speaking.

I must be fearless, unafraid and brave of this unknown.

BE CURIOUS OF THE UNKNOWN

RATHER THAN FEARED OF IT

She was not just fragile, soft, gentle and kind,

she had been tested many times,

and challenged her stars,

her life accutely so refined,

but there was still the question,

what was out there for her to find,

she knew adventure would find her,

but continue to look within,

for she was the finest eulogy

to a beautiful, bright mind.

Atlas

You can only mask your pain for so long,
you can only disguise what you feel
until your virtue is lost,
do not be ashamed of your fire.
The map is not final,
you can explore whatever you want,
but do so with passion and hunger.

Do we exist to please others?

I don't know,

don't we all demand to be loved at some point?

Are we all expecting too much from this simple life?

Let us be content with the basics for a little while.

Step back and breathe.

You can't starve yourself of energy,

you can't soak in the sun and be ablaze for everyone to see,

your light is your power,

but in order to stay bright,

you need time

to be free with the stars for a moment or two,

breathe in that oxygen

and taste the simpleness of just being alive.

The toughest truth

is that you can't expect to go through life

without being hurt or feel some kind of suffering.

In a more artistic way to put it;

you have to flirt with pain in order to conquer it.

Just make sure to respect yourself enough to fight back.

Throw your voice into the stars,

and accept your journey will not be so neat,

be rare like stardust in the day,

and shatter all doubt that makes you feel incomplete,

let your voice be heard, far and wide,

your stories need telling, after so much defeat,

how you have battled through adversity,

on and on, in confidence you repeat,

even with good morals,

your attitude was so elite,

you remained consistence and precise,

look back on your problems,

for all that you have beat.

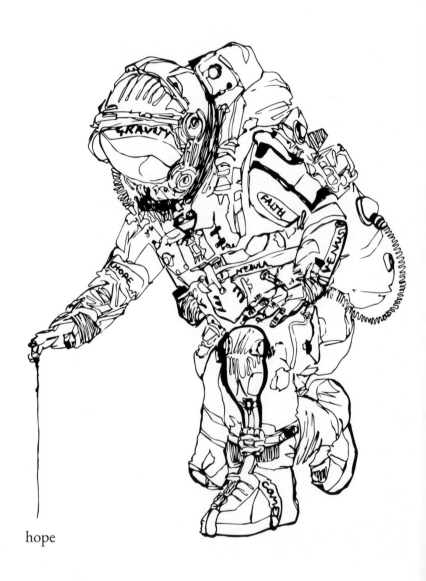

hope

Sometimes, you've got to look back at what hurt you to heal from the bruises they left on you. Both positive and negative, everything you have done, and will do, is an experience.

Look at this life as an experiment. Listen to your instinct and listen to your heart, for it says more than you will ever know., express yourself in whatever form you so wish. There is a power in the unknown, the future can be off putting, but try your best not to view it that way. Instead, try look forward to the endless memories and the time spent with yourself and with others. You are more powerful and stronger than you will ever know. The best thing to do is to be grateful, it is the best form of attitude. The best thing I can offer you is this; look forward to the events, activities, meetings, laughs, views, friendships you will make.

This is where your power lies... in your mindset.

This poison inside consumes me,

but I stain my insides with it anyway.

I drink this imaginary poison

for no real reason,

I constantly tell myself it is fictitious,

then it grows a little more,

and by the end of the week,

it has fabricated into something very dark, powerful

and very exhausting.

I can't address it, I let it in, so I should suffer alongside it.

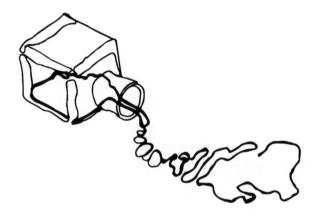

Who am I? I'm being consumed by fire.

I sit alone in a library or in my room on this still night.

The anticipation of who I am going to be is daunting. I

 look and watch other peoples lives like some kind of portal.

I am drawn to it, even though I know it isn't healthy for me.

I don't feel relevant

or I feel that my presence is but a shadow in others lives.

I don't feel impactful and these afternoons turn to evenings;

they are lonely and hollow.

I have lost my identity and there is a knot in my stomach,

a nervous knot. Who am I?

Anything I want to be I can be.

These emotions are just temporary.

They are but stardust sweeping through,

I am more than temporary, I am more than these nerves.

I am an illustrator of dreams, an architect of art.

This pain is a myth,

I am ready to start anew and conquer the source of this rotting,

I am ready to get to putting this fire out,

and getting to the bottom of this brokenness.

FALL DOWN SEVEN TIMES, STAND UP EIGHT.

She is a constellation of beauty,

a nebula of elegance,

she is an enigma,

from somewhere between the sand and the stardust,

she makes me believe in something greater,

greater than myself,

tell me I'm forever yours.

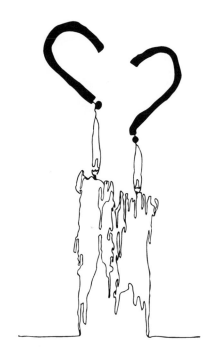

In an age where beauty is considered over intellect,
and in a time where fame is considered over talent
respect is no longer earned but bought,
depression really is inevitable for a lot of people.

I'd sail away just to follow you

i'd chase the dream across the blue

'cause I am rich no matter what I lose

i'd rather risk it all and find the truth

it's all because of our love,

all because of, our love,

i'm gonna change my heart

and start anew

and turn myself into someone new

if I can't be the one I choose

i'd rather leave it all

and die with you

it's all because of our love

all because of our love

TIM BERGLING (AVICII)

The collateral damage of the surgeries

have left me wounded and desperate.

Desperate to escape pain and anxiety.

It has a supernova impression on my fragile state of mind

and I have never felt like a longing like this one.

I am not myself anymore

and that is the damage that has stoned me

with the anxiety that kicks in at any moment.

It fills me up.

The worry sinks in and the panic attacks begin

and it feels like panic shatters my bones...

I have nothing left to give

and sit absorbing this inner pain like some pathetic sponge...

I have nothing left to give

but pour it all into my work...

What makes you a success in this world
is not by how many material possessions you own,
but by how how many souls you've set afire.

If society was to crumble,

if the pavements erupted

and the streets fell silent,

if the world started over anew,

would we find each other?

Would we discover ourselves as we are now?

Or would we find something else to walk towards?

Admitting being depressed

is like admitting being in the wrong;

it's extremely hard to do

and no one ever enjoys doing so.

But in order to get better,

we must first accept it.

In the end,

I wonder if any of this matters.

In this fraction of time in this vast universe

there is so much wonder.

But we are not, only our stories are lucky enough to be wonders,

and they flash by like the comets we watch in the sky.

So make your story burn like a comets impact on earth.

DEFEND YOUR MIND, AT ALL COSTS

In any case,

in whatever discipline you choose to work on,

you should always be;

consistent as night and day,

as unpredictable as a coastal storm,

and persistent like the oceans waves.

To the beyond.....

Dance daringly in the day,

and sleep deeply through the night,

dream wildly in the evenings

and do not turn your back on the light,

laugh merrily in the mornings,

then rise, rise in peak flight,

hold on to that dream,

and excel, compel with all your might.

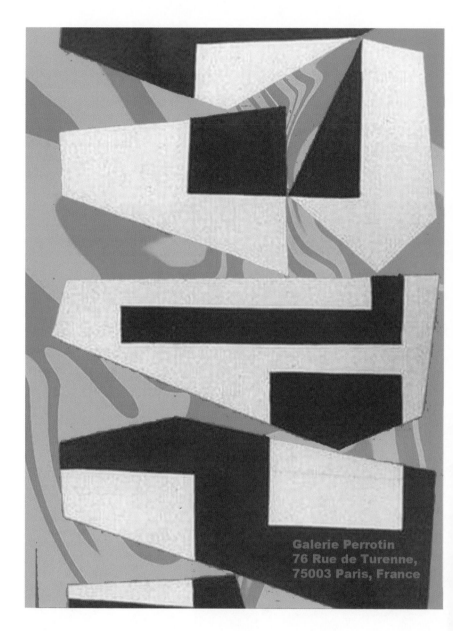

Galerie Perrotin
76 Rue de Turenne,
75003 Paris, France

Sometimes, I am not in any particular mood.

I just feel empty, like a lonely plateau.

I sit up and speak to the stars,

to those planets out there in the distance.

I just want to be forgotten.

But then I listen to myself,

I have to pull myself out of from this longing,

take a lesson from the planets,

they never ask to be seen or appreciated,

but they never take no for an answer,

they are just so consistenly tremendous.

I want to be like one of them,

but I have to be living to feel like that.

We don't create art because it's just good fun.

We do because something instinctively tells us to.

We do it out of passion

and because we need to express ourselves.

Something gets ignited within us

and we have to keep the fire alive.

Perhaps we need to fill in a dark void

and rather than going up in smoke,

our way is to communicate it through art.

Never the less, we need it.

We need art.

We need a way to escape,

break free,

and take flight.

Elegance is a rare commodity,

it's often confused with beauty.

Elegance is how you carry yourself,

it's in how you treat others,

it certainly has nothing to do with money,

and will always mean more than just dressing well.

We all have a little bit of a warrior inside of us.

It takes a great deal of insight to find it,

but when you do, and you will,

you can have a large measure of peace and security,

you can overcome obstacles that you feared

and you will have a new way of life.

I can't put a finger on it...

To talk about the pain,
is painful in itself.
Talking about it just opens up all the wounds,
it's basically saying,
come back and bring the venom back into my thoughts,
it's infectious.
So yes, it is very strenuous to open up again,
but you have to do that in order for you to get better.
Because closing up like a clam,
will only fill the well, the barrier will eventually give way,
you'll crack, shatter and burst.
You'll be a catastrophic supernova
plunging into oblivion,
and that is cold place to suffer,
so we must support each other,
hydrate one another with kindness and love.

I think it's very difficult for me,

I'm naturally an upbeat,

full of energy positive mindset kind of person,

but I enjoy my own company, a time for solace within nature...

but after all these traumas,

I find myself loathing to be alone,

but not for the right reasons.

I get swallowed by my own thoughts and it's a cycle I can't shake.

At times, I think I can't go on,

but then I just keep crossing off another week

and before I know it, it's been 2 months.

I'm finding the war with myself the hardest one I've ever known.

Effulgence - a shining force

It rained stardust all over her,

she glistened in the moonlight,

she became part of the twilight,

she had never felt so alive,

letting radiance pour out of her skin,

she transcended, laughing up at the stars

and in that moment,

felt that time had stopped.

Be a little crazy, a little wild, a little fierce.

Be extreme, dream intensely, create with influence.

If there is a world you want to create, then do it with desire.

Don't be uncertain or precarious,

be absolute and definite.

The world is full of compulsion,

and we must withstand it.

PREVAIL, TRIUMPH, CONQUER

I look down at my scars in search for answers,
and I look to the stars in search of my dreams.
Then I have this instinctive feeling to look within
and find them both resting there.

Somewhere Between The Sand And The Stardust

You can't fit this alone, you have to talk about what is
going through your brain. You need to protect yourself too
from social media and other platforms that are not just addictive,
but also very harmful to us. Our emotions and feelings are
what keep us connected, so make sure to look after those too.

I hope this book gives you inspiration and motivation
in whatever you need it for. With all my love
and gratitude, thank you.

Joshua.

Please seek help, it is worth it, talk and continue your fight....

U.K - https://www.samaritans.org
Call: 116 123

Follow the journey:

www.joshuavanleader.com

Instagram: @joshuavanleader

Joshua Van Leader

Somewhere Between The Sand And The Stardust

Printed in Great Britain
by Amazon

13365110R00125